STORYTELLER: BUDDHIST STORIES

Anita Ganeri

Illustrations by Tracey Fennell

EVANS BROTHERS LIMITED

Introduction

Buddhist Stories

In each of the world's six main religions - Hinduism, Judaism, Buddhism, Christianity, Islam and Sikhism - stories play a very important part. They have been used for many thousands of years to teach people about their faith in a way which makes difficult messages easier to understand. Many stories tell of times in the lives of religious teachers, leaders, gods and goddesses. Others explain mysterious events such as how the world was created or what happens when you die. Many have a strong moral or lesson to teach.

The collection of stories in this book comes from Buddhism. Buddhists follow the teachings of a man called Siddhartha Gautama, who lived in India about 2500 years ago. He saw that there was suffering in the world and tried to find a way to end it. When he found the answer, he became known as the Buddha, or 'one who is awake', because he was able to see things as they really are. Buddhists use his teachings as a guide through their lives. In this book, you can read some of the many stories about the Buddha's life.

STORYTELLER:
BUDDHIST STORIES

Evans Brothers Limited
2a Portman Mansions
Chiltern Street
London W1U 6NR

First published in paperback in 2006

British Library Cataloguing Data
    Ganeri, Anita
    Buddhist stories. – (Storyteller)
    1.Buddhism – Juvenile literature
    I.Title II.Fennell, Tracey
    294.3

    ISBN 0 237 52034 6

Editor: Victoria Brooker
Series Editor: Su Swallow
Designer: Simon Borrough
Illustrations: Tracey Fennell, Allied Artists
Production: Jenny Mulvanny
Consultant: Adiccabandu, Clear Vision Trust

Printed in Malta by Gutenberg Press Ltd.

Acknowledgements
The author and publishers would like to
thank the following for permission to
reproduce copyright material: page 7 The
Bridgeman Art Library/Christie's Images,
page 8 Robert Harding/Ellen Rooney, page
14 Anne & Bury Peerless, page 18 Anne &
Bury Peerless, page 20 Circa Photo
Library/John Smith, page 21 Circa Photo
Library, page 23 Circa Photo
Library/William Holtby, page 26 The
Bridgeman Art Library, page 28 Robert
Harding/Rolf Richardson

VISIT OUR WEBSITE
Evans
www.evansbooks.co.uk

Contents

The Birth of the Buddha

Long ago, King Suddhodana and his wife Queen Maya ruled a small kingdom in the north of India. They lived in a magnificent palace in the beautiful city of Kapilavastu, the capital of the kingdom.

One night, Queen Maya had a dream. She dreamt that she saw a dazzling light shining down from the sky, and out of the light came a pure white elephant with a lotus blossom in its trunk. When Queen Maya woke up, she remembered her dream and was filled with joy. But what did her dream mean? The king summoned four wise men to the palace and asked them to explain.

"Oh, your majesties," the wise men said. "This is wonderful news indeed. For the Queen will soon have a baby son who will grow up to be very great and good. Rejoice, rejoice and be happy!"

When the time came for her baby to be born, Queen Maya set off for her father's home in the next-door kingdom. This was the custom at the time. On the way, she stopped to rest in the beautiful garden of Lumbini, which was filled with flowers, and fruit trees, birds and bees. There she gave birth to her son.

It was a clear May night and the Moon shone round and full in the sky. Angels wrapped the baby in a fine, soft shawl and showered him with sweet-smelling rose

petals. Then a rumbling earthquake shook the Earth and the world was flooded with light. The trees in the garden burst into bloom. Throughout the land, there was a great feeling of peace and joyfulness as people forgot their worries. For this was no ordinary baby. ▶

Did you know?

Wesak is an important Buddhist festival which happens on the day of the full Moon in May. The festival remembers the Buddha's birth, his enlightenment and passing away. Buddhists visit the temple and decorate their homes with flowers and lamps. Some send Wesak cards to their friends. It is a day for being especially kind and generous to others.

7

There was great rejoicing in Kapilavastu when Queen Maya returned. The king and queen named the baby Siddhartha, which means the one who brings about good.

One day, shortly after Siddhartha's birth, an old man called Asita visited the palace. He had travelled for days to see the baby. Now Asita was known to be a great teacher, famous for his wisdom and holiness. He looked at the baby for a very long time, then, to the dismay of the king and queen, he began to cry.

"Whatever is the matter, wise Asita?" asked the worried king. "We love our son dearly, please say what is wrong."

"Don't be afraid," Asita said. "Your son will grow up to become a very great man. See the light shining from his fingers. This is just one of the special signs. A choice of fate waits for him in life. He might become a mighty ruler, the greatest king in history. Or he might be a great and wise teacher, showing people how to live in peace and love. I am crying not because anything is wrong, but because I am already a very old man. I am sad that I will not live to learn from him."

Then Asita took one last, long look at the baby and turned and left the palace.

Did you know?

For Buddhists, lotus flowers are very special. Lotuses grow in muddy water. But their flowers rise to the surface to bloom. This is like a human being, full of faults and failings, who grows into a better person by following the Buddha's teachings. You start off as a half-closed bud. But by being kind and loving to others, you too can grow and flower.

Siddhartha and the Swan

In his father's palace, Siddhartha grew up to be loving, caring and kind-hearted. He was so good at his lessons that his teachers could not keep up with him. He soon knew more than they did. He also learned to shoot with a bow and arrow, and to fight with a sword. For King Suddhodana remembered the wise man's words. He wanted Siddhartha to be a great king and rule after him, and these were the skills a brave king would need. But when lessons were over, Siddhartha was often to be found in the palace gardens, watching the birds and animals.

One day, Siddhartha was sitting by the lake when a flock of white swans flew overhead. Suddenly, one of the swans fell from the sky and landed at Siddhartha's feet. An arrow was stuck in its wing.

"Poor swan," said Siddhartha, "I'll look after you. Don't be afraid."

Very gently, he pulled out the arrow and wrapped the wounded swan in his own shirt to keep it warm.

Just then, his cousin, Devadatta, came running up in great excitement. He was carrying a bow and some arrows.

"What are you doing?" he shouted at Siddhartha. "That's my swan, not yours. I shot it fair and square. Now, give it back, or else."

But Siddhartha refused and so the two boys began to argue. They quarrelled and quarrelled but neither would give in. Finally, they decided to go to the king and let him decide who was right. ▶

The king and his ministers listened carefully to their story. First, Devadatta described what had happened. Then Siddhartha had his say. Now who did the swan belong to?

"Devadatta shot the swan so it is his," one minister said.

"But Siddhartha found the swan so it is his," said another.

Even the ministers could not decide.

" I can help you," said a quavering voice. Everyone turned round. There in the doorway stood a very old man whom nobody had ever seen before. "No one wants to feel pain or die, and it's just the same for animals," he said. "Give the swan to the boy who tried to save its life, not to the boy who would kill it."

So Siddhartha was allowed to keep the swan and he cared for it until it was well again. Then he took it down to the lake in the palace garden and let it fly away to join its friends.

Did you know?

Not harming living things is the first of five precepts or promises which Buddhists follow in their daily lives. They are:

1. Not harming or killing living things but helping others.
2. Not stealing or taking things you are not given but being generous.
3. Not being greedy but being content.
4. Not telling lies or speaking unkindly but telling the truth.
5. Not drinking or taking drugs but keeping a clear mind.

Did you know?

Being kind to animals is very important for Buddhists. They believe that animals have feelings too. Not only should you not hurt them but you should try to do your best for them, as Siddhartha does in the story. This means being kind to your pet, for example, or putting a spider outside instead of killing it.

The Four Sights

Siddhartha lived in his father's palace, surrounded by the finest and best of everything. King Suddhodana wanted his son to become a great king so much that he kept him shielded from the world outside. For if Siddhartha ever saw the grief and suffering in the world, he might choose to leave the palace behind and become a great teacher, as wise Asita had foretold.

Siddhartha married a princess from a neighbouring kingdom whose name was Yasodhara. He won the right to marry her in an archery contest by firing an arrow from a bow so heavy that no one else could lift it. The king gave his son three beautiful palaces as a wedding present, one for each season of the year. Siddhartha seemed to have everything his heart desired.

Even so, Siddhartha often felt restless and bored. He felt sure that there must be more to life than wealth and luxury. Then, when he was about 29 years old, his life changed for ever. One day, he asked his charioteer, Channa, to take him for a ride in the countryside. Channa chose four fine, lotus-white horses and harnessed them to a magnificent chariot. Then they drove out of the palace gates.

They had not gone far before Siddhartha noticed a very old man by the wayside, his body hunched and bent. He was supporting himself on a walking stick. Siddhartha was shocked at what he saw.

"Who is that man?" Siddhartha asked Channa, "and what is wrong with him? Why is his skin so dry and wrinkled, and his body so thin and bent?"

"He is just an old man, master," Channa replied. "It happens to us all. You, me, your wife, Yasodhara, we are all growing older all the time."

Siddhartha thought hard about what he had seen as he rode back to his father's palace.

Next day, Siddhartha and Channa rode out again. This time they saw a sick man whose body was wracked with pain. He was so weak he could not stand up but lay groaning on the ground. ▶

"Look, Channa!" called Siddhartha. "Who is that poor man and why is he shaking and crying so pitifully?"

"He is just a sick man, master," Channa replied.

"You must not worry. Everyone feels ill sometimes."

Siddhartha was horrified. He ordered Channa to take him back to the palace so that he could ponder what he had seen. It made him feel very sad.

But worse was to come when they rode out again the next day. Further down the road, they passed a group of mourners weeping as they followed the funeral procession behind a corpse.

"Channa, why is that man lying so still?" asked Siddhartha. "Is he asleep? And why are those people crying?"

Once again, Channa explained.

"The man is dead, master," he said, "and those people are his family and friends. They are sad that he is gone. But they know that there is nothing they can do. Death comes to everyone. We will all die one day."

Back in the comfort of the palace, Siddhartha thought long and hard about all the suffering and unhappiness he had seen for the first time in his life.

"But what is the point then," he said sadly, "of being born at all, if old age, sickness and death are all we have to look forward to?"

This time Channa did not know the answer.

The following day, Channa harnessed the horses to the chariot once more, and drove Siddhartha out of the palace. Some time later, a poor monk came wandering by. His head was shaven and his feet were bare. All he had with him was the orange robe he wore and the bowl in his hand. But on his face he wore a look of great peace and thoughtfulness.

"How happy he looks," said Siddhartha, "even though he has nothing. Who do you think he is, Channa?"

"Master, he is a holy man," answered Channa. "He has seen the suffering of the world - the old age, sickness and death. And he has left his home and possessions behind to search for a way to true happiness. All he owns is the robe he is wearing and a bowl for food."

"At last I know what to do," thought Siddhartha. "I shall be like this holy man. I shall leave my home and belongings, and search for a way to end the suffering I have seen." ▶

Later that night, Siddhartha returned to the palace and told Channa to saddle his favourite horse. Silently, so as not to wake them, he said goodbye to his sleeping wife and their newborn son. Then he and Channa rode quietly out the palace, and on and on until they reached the river. Here Siddhartha took off his fine, silk clothes and swapped them for a beggar's patched robes. Then he took his sword and cut off his long, black hair. Softly he said goodbye to Channa.

"My trusty Channa," he said. "Take my clothes and horse back to the palace and tell my father and wife that I have gone. Tell them not to worry. One day I will return to teach them what I know. But, for now, I must say goodbye."

Did you know?

Some Buddhists follow the Buddha's example and leave their homes and possessions behind. They become monks and nuns. They spend their lives teaching and meditating. Their simple robes and shaved heads are signs that they have given up their worldly ties and devoted themselves to the Buddha's teachings. Like all Buddhists, they know that the way to happiness is through living a simple life, being kind and thoughtful and not harming others.

Did you know?

The first three sights showed Siddhartha that suffering and unhappiness are facts of life which happen to everyone. The fourth sight showed him the importance of searching for the truth. Everyone falls ill sometimes; everyone gets old and one day, everyone will die. You cannot stop this happening but you can rise above it by using the four sights to help you remember how important life is.

14

The Search for the Truth

When Channa had gone, Siddhartha crossed the river, ready to start his new life. But how would he find the answers he was seeking? Where should he look for them first? Dressed in simple robes and eating only the food he could beg, he set off into the forest. He had heard of two great teachers of meditation. Perhaps they could show him a way to end suffering. But Siddhartha quickly learned everything the wise men could teach him, and one day they said they could teach him no more. Still he had not found the answer.

So Siddhartha continued his travels. Next he went to live with a group of holy men whose way of life was very hard. For six long years, Siddhartha stayed with them. He wore clothes so rough they made his skin sore and went without washing for months on end. He spent hours and hours without moving a muscle, standing or squatting with one arm over his head. In summer, he sat for hours in the burning sun. In winter, he bathed in icy water. He ate so little and grew so thin that he could feel his spine through the skin of his stomach.

But still the answers did not come in his search for the truth about life. Finally, one day, so weak and exhausted that he could hardly stand, he left the forest and made his way to the banks of a nearby river. Here he bathed in the water and ate a meal of milk and rice, given to him by a kindly girl. He knew that he must find another way to the truth. That evening, strengthened by his meal, he sat down, cross-legged, beneath a fine, tall tree.

"I shall not move from here until I see the truth," he said. "however long it may take." ▶

Then he closed his eyes and began to meditate.

All through the night, Siddhartha sat in deep meditation, perfectly deep and perfectly quiet. But he was not left in peace. Mara, the evil one, did not want Siddhartha to succeed in his search. For Mara spread hatred, greed and ignorance. If Siddhartha discovered an end to suffering, Mara's power would be destroyed. So he and his evil forces tried to tempt Siddhartha from his search for the truth.

First, Mara summoned up a dreadful storm, strong enough to destroy a town, and hurled it at Siddhartha. But it faded away before it touched him. Next, he sent a downpour of torrential rain but not a drop touched Siddhartha's robes. Ever more desperate, Mara sounded a great, booming drum and summoned his evil army of evil spirits, demons and goblins.

"Attack!" he screeched. "Attack!"

With a blood-curdling scream, the demons and goblins ran towards Siddhartha but still he sat calmly beneath the tree. They hurled burning spears at him, and poisoned arrows, but they all fell as petals at his feet. Nothing could hurt Siddhartha.

Mara had one last trick up his sleeve.

"Why are you wasting your time like this?" he wheedled. "Go back to your palace. Don't you miss your beautiful wife and son? Don't you miss your fine clothes and food?" ▶

Did you know?

Meditation means training your mind so that it becomes calm and still. This is very important in Buddhism. Buddhists believe that meditating will bring them closer to enlightenment. They meditate on their own or in groups. Learning to meditate takes lots of practice.

Did you know?

The tree under which the Buddha gained enlightenment is called the bodhi tree, or tree of awakening. It was a type of fig tree. Enlightenment means seeing the truth behind things, or seeing things as they really are. Buddhists hope that, by following the Buddha's teachings, they too will achieve enlightenment.

Of course, Siddhartha missed his family but he could not let Mara tempt him to go back. He ignored Mara's sneering words. Calmly, he reached out his hand and touched the Earth to call it up as his strength and support. And, as if to reply, the earth shook beneath him and Mara fled in terror.

As the long night drew on, Siddhartha at last found the answers he had been looking for. Suddenly he saw the truth. It was like waking up from a long, deep sleep. Now he knew why people suffered, why they fell ill, got old and died. And now he knew how to help them to see the truth for themselves and find happiness and peace. For Siddhartha Gautama had become the Buddha, the awakened one, who had seen through suffering to the truth.

Did you know?

Bodh Gaya is the place in India where the Buddha gained enlightenment. Buddhists come here from all over the world to visit the Mahabodhi Temple and its great golden image of the Buddha. The bodhi tree in Bodh Gaya is said to have grown from the original tree under which the Buddha meditated.

The Buddha's First Teaching

For many more days, and many more nights, the Buddha sat beneath the tree, meditating on what he had learned. He was filled with great happiness, free from all worry and pain. Two passing merchants brought him food to eat and became his first followers. When they had gone, the Buddha wondered what to do next. Should he go and teach other people what he knew? Would they be able to understand? Or should he keep his thoughts to himself? Then, in his mind's eye, he saw the world as if it were a lotus pond.

"Some people are like unopened lotus buds, while others are ready to open up their petals. Some people will be ready for my teaching. Others will not," he said.

So the Buddha set off for the holy city of Varanasi, and after many days of travelling, he reached the Deer Park which lay nearby. There he knew he would find the five holy men who had been his companions in the forest. He wanted to teach them first.

But when they saw him coming, they whispered among themselves.

"Let's ignore him," they said. "After all, he abandoned us once before. Let him sit down but don't talk to him."

But as the Buddha came closer, they saw that something special had happened to him. Forgetting their plan to ignore him, they made him sit down with them, took his robe and bowl and brought him some water to drink. That evening, the Buddha gave his first teaching. It was called the Turning of the Wheel of Law.

"To discover the truth, you must realise four truths about life," he told the holy men. "The first is that human life is full of suffering. And the reason for this is because people are greedy. They always want something more. But there is also an end to suffering and a way to find peace ▶

19

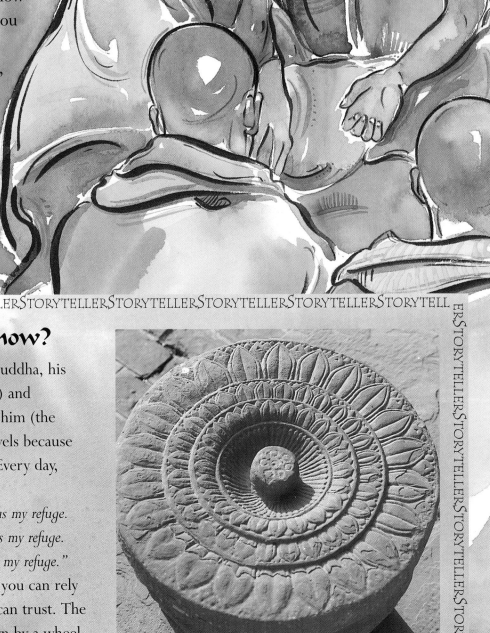

beyond words. It is called the middle path."

"But how do we follow the path?" the holy men asked.

"There are eight steps on the path," replied the Buddha, "Of right understanding, right attitude, right speech, right action, right work, right effort, right mindfulness and right meditation. Follow these and they will lead you to enlightenment."

And with these words, the five holy men finally saw the truth, just as the Buddha had done. And for the rest of his

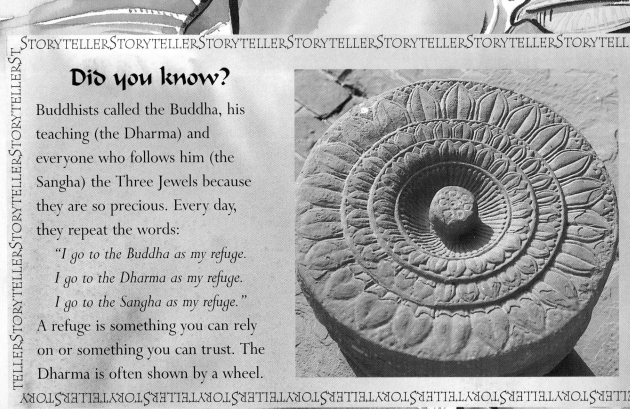

Did you know?

Buddhists called the Buddha, his teaching (the Dharma) and everyone who follows him (the Sangha) the Three Jewels because they are so precious. Every day, they repeat the words:

I go to the Buddha as my refuge.
I go to the Dharma as my refuge.
I go to the Sangha as my refuge."

A refuge is something you can rely on or something you can trust. The Dharma is often shown by a wheel.

long life, the Buddha travelled all over India, teaching princes and poor people alike. Many people came to hear him and to join his band of followers. And they helped spread his message far and wide.

Did you know?

Buddhists believe that, when you die, you are born again. It is like a never-ending cycle of birth, death and rebirth. What you are like in your next life depends on your actions in this life. Good actions may lead to future happiness; bad actions lead to unhappiness. Buddhists believe that, by following the Buddha's teachings, you can break free of this cycle and find perfect peace. Buddhist monks devote their lives to studying the Buddha's teachings.

The Story of Kisagotami

There was once a woman called Kisagotami. She was married to a wealthy merchant and for a while she was very happy. But when her only son was just a year old, he fell ill and died. Kisagotami was broken hearted. In her grief, she went from door to door, asking for medicine for her son which would bring him back to life again. Some people ignored her. Others laughed behind her back. Then one day, she met a wise man who felt sorry for her plight.

"Go and see the Buddha, Kisagotami," he told her. "Perhaps he will be able to help you."

So Kisagotami went to the Buddha, still holding her child in her arms.

"I beg you, Lord Buddha," she wept. "Please help me bring my son back to life."

"I will help you, Kisagotami," the Buddha said gently, for he saw how unhappy she was. "But first you must go into the town and bring me a mustard seed from a house where no one has died."

Kisagotami hurried into the town and stopped at the very first house she saw.

"I have to fetch a mustard seed," she said. "From a house where no one has died."

"I'm sorry," came the reply. "You can have a mustard seed with pleasure. But my grandmother died last year."

Everywhere she went, the answer was the same. Everyone wanted to help her but they could not. In every house she visited, someone had died. And now she understood

She took her little son to be buried. Then at the end of the day, she returned to the Buddha.

"Have you got the mustard seed?" the Buddha asked.

"No," Kisagotami said, smiling. "But now I see that I am not alone in my sorrow. Everything changes - it is part of life. And death must come to everyone sooner or later."

Then Kisagotami became a follower of the Buddha and set out to learn the truth about life.

Did you know?

Many people came to the Buddha for help with their problems. The Buddha was always kind and caring. He listened to everyone and knew what to do. Buddhists called this loving kindness metta. It is one of the four best qualities a person can have. The others are compassion, being pleased for others and calmly accepting whatever may happen.

Did you know?

When Buddhists worship, they place flowers on a shrine in front of an image of the Buddha. At first the flowers look fresh and colourful but eventually they fade and die. This is a reminder of the Buddha's teaching that nothing lasts for ever. Everything is always changing. This is sometimes sad, as in the story, but it also means that everyone can change for the better.

Angulimala, the Robber

Long ago, there lived a terrible robber called Angulimala, a fearsome name meaning "finger necklace". For Angulimala was not content to steal. He had made a promise to rob and kill a thousand people, and, to keep count, he cut off their fingers to wear on a cord around his neck.

No one could catch Angulimala. He was very cunning and enormously strong, and could run faster than the fastest horse. If the king sent his soldiers after him, Angulimala killed them all and added their fingers to his gruesome necklace. No wonder people were terrified and did not dare go out at night.

One day, the Buddha heard the people talking about Angulimala and how they wanted to get rid of him once and for all. Without saying anything, the Buddha set off along the road towards the den where the robber lived.

"Don't go that way," warned a passer-by. "If Angulimala catches you, he'll kill you for certain."

Still the Buddha walked quietly on his way. Soon he was the only traveller on that stretch of road. From his den, Angulimala saw him coming.

"What a fool!" the robber sneered. "He can't have heard of my reputation. Never mind. Let him come. I'll soon add his finger to my necklace. He! he! he!"

Then wicked Angulimala picked up his sword and started to chase the Buddha down the road. But a strange thing happened. However fast Angulimala ran, he could not catch the Buddha. The Buddha was always just out of his reach. Stranger still, the Buddha was not even running. He was walking along as normal.

Angulimala got crosser and crosser, and more and more out of breath. He ran and ran, until he could run no further.

"Stop!" he panted. "Stop, I tell you, and stand still!"

"I have stopped," replied the Buddha, calmly, as he kept on walking. "It is you who are moving and I who am still."

"What do you mean?" shouted the robber. Surely things were the other way round? ▶

Then the Buddha explained. Although his legs were still moving, his mind was calm and still. But Angulimala's mind was racing with hatred and anger, even though he was standing still. The Buddha's words touched the tiny patch of goodness still left in the robber's black heart. He took his sword and flung it into a ditch. Then he fell on his knees and begged the Buddha to help him and teach him how to meditate.

And that is the story of how the terrible robber, Angulimala, become one of the Buddha's most trusted monks.

Did you know?

Many of the stories about the Buddha come from a collection of writings called the Tripitaka, which means 'three baskets'. The first basket has rules for monks. The second has the Buddha's teachings and stories about his life. The third explains his teachings. The most popular part of the Tripitaka is the Dhammapada, a collection of the Buddha's sayings.

The Buddha Passes Away

When the Buddha was about eighty years old, he knew that the time was coming for him to leave the world. He called Ananda, his faithful and constant companion, to him.

"I have taught you all I know, Ananda," he said. "Now I am old. When I am gone, let my teachings be your guide. They will light you through your life."

Then the Buddha called his monks together and began his very last journey, to the little town of Kushinagara. On the way, they stopped to rest ▶

in a mango grove. Chunda, the blacksmith, came to see them and invited them to his home for a meal. The blacksmith went to a great deal of trouble for his honoured guests.

After the meal, the Buddha fell ill with a fever and terrible pains. Still he travelled on to Kushinagara. Just outside the town, he stopped to rest in a grove of trees. There he lay down, worn out by his journey.

Seeing his friend and teacher so weak and ill, Ananda was filled with grief.

"What shall we do without you?" he said, and began to sob bitterly.

"Do not be sad, dear Ananda," the Buddha told him. "You have been a king among kings. Remember the teaching - everything changes and passes away. Now go and strive diligently."

Then the Buddha passed away and reached the perfect peace of nirvana. And, as the monks mourned, the trees scattered petals over his body.

Did you know?

Today there are over 400 million Buddhists all over the world. Many still live in Asia where Buddhism began. Buddhism has also spread to Europe and the USA where there are many Buddhists temples and monasteries. All Buddhists use the Buddha's teaching as a guide for how to live their lives.

STORYTELLERSTORYTELLERSTORYTELLERST

Did you know?

When Buddhists worship, they show their respect for the Buddha. They light candles and offer flowers and incense to an image of the Buddha. This is called puja. They also read the holy books and meditate. Some Buddhist have a small shrine at home. Some visit the temple for puja led by the monks.

28

Glossary

Ananda The Buddha's chief follower and his close friend. He was also the Buddha's cousin.

Bodh Gaya A town in India where the Buddha gained enlightenment. Today Buddhists come from all over the world to visit the town.

Buddha A name which means 'enlightened one'. It was given to a man called Siddhartha Gautama who lived in India about 2500 years ago.

Buddhism A way of life based on the teachings of the Buddha. People who follow these teachings are called Buddhists.

Devadatta The Buddha's cousin who later plotted to kill the Buddha but his plot failed.

Dhammapada A collection of the Buddha's sayings. It is part of the sacred Buddhist writings called the Tripitaka.

Dharma The name for the Buddha's teachings.

Enlightenment Seeing things as they really are and understanding the truth about things.

Five precepts Five promises which Buddhists try to keep in their daily lives.

Four sights The four sights which the Buddha saw - the old man, the sick man, the dead man and the monk. They made him give up his old life and search for an end to suffering.

Lotus A plant which grows in rivers and ponds. Its flowers come to the surface to bloom.

Mara The evil one who tried to tempt the Buddha away from his search for the truth.

Maya, Queen The Buddha's mother

Meditation A way of training your mind so that it becomes still and calm. It is very important in Buddhism.

Metta A Buddhist word for loving kindness. This is one of the best qualities a person can have.

Monks Men who give up their homes and possessions to devote themselves to the Buddha's teachings.

Nirvana A state of perfect peace and happiness which Buddhists try to achieve.

Nuns Women who give up their homes and possessions to devote themselves to the Buddha's teachings.

Puja A Buddhist word for worship. When Buddhists worship, they offer gifts of flowers, candles and incense to the Buddha to show their respect.

Sangha Everyone who follows the Buddha

Siddhartha Gautama The name of the Buddha before he gained enlightenment

Suddhodana, King The Buddha's father

Three Jewels The Buddha, the Dharma and the Sangha. They are so precious to Buddhists that they call them jewels.

Tripitaka A collection of sacred Buddhist writings. It has rules for monks, the Buddha's teachings and stories about the Buddha's life.

Wesak The festival when Buddhists remember the Buddha's birth, enlightenment and passing away (death). It happens in May.

Yasodhara The Buddha's wife

Index

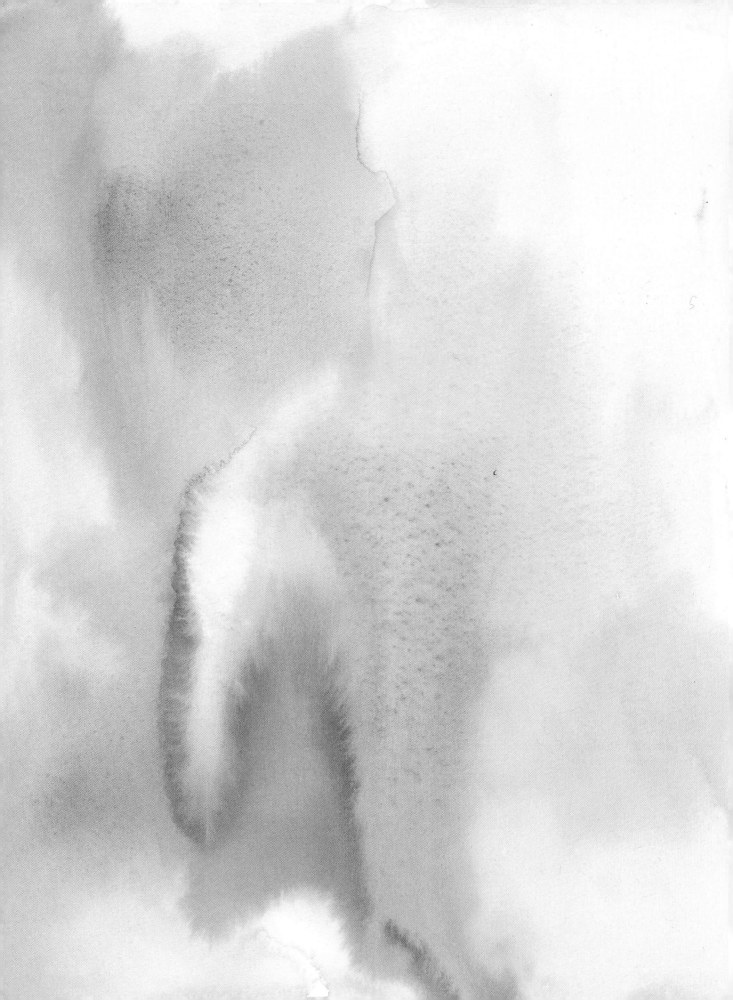